DATE DUE

# Science Matters
# LEVERS

## Jennifer Howse

WEIGL PUBLISHERS INC.

**Published by Weigl Publishers Inc.**
350 5ᵗʰ Avenue, Suite 3304, PMB 6G
New York, NY USA 10118-0069
Website: www.weigl.com

### Library of Congress Cataloging-in-Publication Data

Howse, Jennifer.
Levers / Jennifer Howse.
    p. cm. -- (Science matters)
Includes index.
ISBN 978-1-60596-031-9 (hard cover : alk. paper) -- ISBN 978-1-60596-032-6 (soft cover : alk. paper)
1. Levers--Juvenile literature. 2. Lifting and carrying--Juvenile literature. I. Title.
TJ147.H72 2009
621.8--dc22

                                    2009001921


Printed in China
1 2 3 4 5 6 7 8 9 13 12 11 10 09


**Editor** Nick Winnick
**Design and Layout** Terry Paulhus

**Photograph Credits**

Weigl acknowledges Getty Images as its primary photo supplier for this title.
Kenzie Browne: Page 5.

All of the Internet URLs given in the book were valid at the time of publication. However, due to the dynamic nature of the Internet, some addresses may have changed, or sites may have ceased to exist since publication. While the author and publisher regret any inconvenience this may cause readers, no responsibility for any such changes can be accepted by either the author or the publisher.

Every reasonable effort has been made to trace ownership and to obtain permission to reprint copyright material. The publishers would be pleased to have any errors or omissions brought to their attention so that they may be corrected in subsequent printings.

# Contents

# What is a Lever?

Levers can be found all around you. When people use a nutcracker or hit a baseball, they are using types of levers. Levers are even used for fishing. Both fishing rods and oars are levers.

A lever is a moveable bar that rests on a solid point called the **fulcrum**. Pushing, pulling, and lifting are common types of work. These can be made easier using levers.

■ A lever is one of six simple machines. People use simple machines to make daily tasks easier.

# Parts of a Lever

**There are two important parts that a lever needs in order to work. They are the bar and fulcrum.**

The first piece a lever needs to work properly is called the bar. It is a long, **rigid** structure that supports the **load** and the **effort**. The load is the object to be moved. The effort is the push or pull that is used to move the load.

The second important part of a lever is the fulcrum. When effort is placed on the bar, the bar moves against the fulcrum. The fulcrum changes the direction of the push or pull, and moves the load.

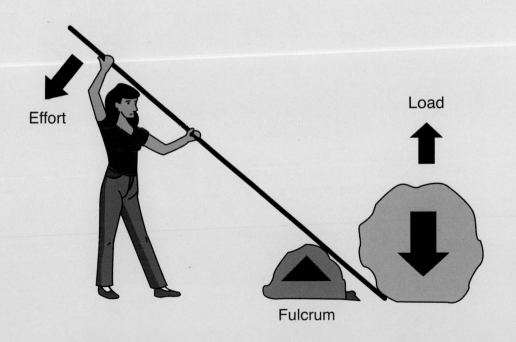

Effort

Load

Fulcrum

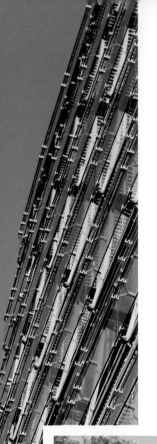

# How do Levers Work?

Levers change the amount of force needed to move a load. For example, a lever can be used to lift a heavy object such as a milk crate. The end of a long wooden board can be placed under the crate. The board acts as a bar. A solid object, such as a cement block, can be placed under the board near the crate. This acts as the fulcrum. Pushing on the long end of the board will lift the crate easily.

■ The distance a board needs to be pushed to move an object changes if the fulcrum is moved.

# Input and Output

**Two important forces are involved in moving a lever. They are called input and output.**

Input is the effort that is used to move the lever. Output is the force that moves the load. Input and output are always equal when a lever is moved.

For example, when the fulcrum is close to the load, the opposite end of the bar must move a long way in order to move the load a little way. This means that the load moves a short distance, but with a great deal of force. The opposite end of the bar moves a long way, but with a little force.

Work is the total of the distance an object moves and the force used on it. Moving a large distance with a little force is the same amount of work as moving a little distance with a large force.

# Lever Laws

The ancient Greeks were the first to discover how levers worked. A scientist named Archimedes came up with the Law of **Equilibrium** to describe the kind of balance that lets levers work.

The Law of Equilibrium uses **mathematics** to find out how hard a person would have to push one side of a lever to move the other side a certain distance.

■ Many discoveries made by ancient Greek scientists, such as Archimedes, are still useful today.

# A Life of Science

**Ancient Greek scientists were some of the first people to write about force and motion. Archimedes was one of these scientists.**

Archimedes lived more than 2,200 years ago. He had many questions about how simple machines worked, but he is best-known for his work on levers.

After studying for a long time, Archimedes felt he knew a great deal about equilibrium. He told a Greek king that, with a long enough lever, he could move Earth.

The king wanted proof that a lever could be so strong. He asked Archimedes to move a heavy load from a ship to a dock. Archimedes set up a lever and easily moved the load without help.

# Long-lasting Levers

Levers are one of the oldest tools used by humans. Many structures throughout history have been built with the help of levers.

People used levers to help move building materials that were too heavy to move by hand. Ancient wonders of the world, such as the Colosseum in Rome, were built with the help of simple machines such as levers and **inclined planes**.

Scientists believe that the ancient Egyptians used simple levers to build the pyramids. These are huge triangle-shaped tombs built of stone. The ancient Greeks also used levers in art and construction.

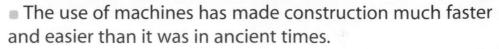
The use of machines has made construction much faster and easier than it was in ancient times.

# Stone-Age Levers

**A ring of stones stands on the Salisbury Plain in Great Britain. These stones are called Stonehenge.**

Stonehenge was built more than 5,000 years ago. People brought 82 giant stones from Wales to the site of Stonehenge. These stones traveled 240 miles (386 kilometers) before they were placed in circles on the Salisbury Plain. Some of the stones weigh 44 tons (40 tonnes) or more.

These people needed a way to set the stones in place easily. Some of the tools they used were levers. Scientists think these levers were likely long tree trunks. Large stones were used as fulcrums. Using these simple levers, people moved the heavy stones upright.

# Lever Types

There are three different types of lever. Each is useful for doing a different kind of task.

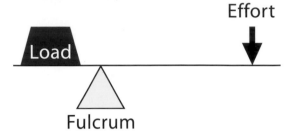

A first-class lever has the fulcrum in the middle of the bar. The load and effort are at opposite ends of the bar. A seesaw is an example of a first-class lever.

A second-class lever has the fulcrum at the end of the bar. The load is in the middle of the bar, and the effort is at the opposite end. A wheelbarrow is an example of a second-class lever.

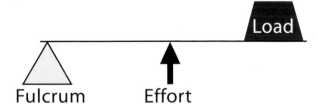

A third-class lever has the fulcrum at the end of the bar. The effort is in the middle of the bar, and the load is at the opposite end. A fishing rod is an example of a third-class lever.

# Levers at Work

### A Hammer Claw

The claw of a hammer is a first-class lever. The hammer claw is used to pull nails out of a board. The claw is placed under the head of a nail, and effort is applied to the handle. The hammer head acts as a fulcrum, and the claw pulls the nail upward.

### Nutcracker

A nutcracker is two second-class levers joined at the fulcrum. The fulcrum is the hinge at the front of the nutcracker. The nut between the two bars is the load. The force comes from the handles being squeezed together.

### Baseball Bat

A baseball ball is a third-class lever. For a right-handed batter, the left hand becomes the fulcrum when the bat is swung. The right hand provides the **power** of the swing. When the bat connects with the ball, the ball becomes the load to be moved.

# Complex Machines

Complex machines are made up of more than one simple machine. They might include any of the six simple machines, including levers.

Complex machines combine simple machines because they each have different useful properties. Complex machines can have a greater **mechanical advantage** than simple ones.

■ An oil pump is a type of complex machine that acts as a lever.

# Bicycles

**There is one bicycle for every two people on Earth. Other than walking, it is the most common way humans move from place to place.**

A bicycle is a complex machine. It is made up of many simple machines, such as levers, wheels, and **pulleys**.

Levers are an important piece of safety gear on a bike. The brakes on the handlebars are levers. When the brake handles are squeezed, that force moves to the brake pads. The brake pads push against the wheels and stop the bike.

# Modern Levers

Levers have been used for thousands of years. In modern times, levers are combined with other simple machines to make more powerful building tools. Levers are an important part of many modern building machines, including power shovels and cranes. These levers often use **hydraulics**. Hydraulic levers can lift very heavy loads.

■ Shovels used in construction are able to move with the use of hydraulics.

# Levers On High

**Cranes are very large levers. Often, they are used in construction.**

Cranes can be seen in the skyline of almost any city. Construction of tall buildings is greatly helped by these machines. The beam running across the top of a crane is a type of first class lever.

A heavy load is lifted by a cable attached to the shorter end of the lever. The force which winds the cable is applied on the long end of the lever. This makes it much easier to lift heavy building materials to the top floors of a construction site.

# Gaining an Advantage

There are six simple machines. They are *inclined planes*, *levers*, *pulleys*, *screws*, *wedges*, and the *wheel and axle*. All simple machines are designed to make work easier. These machines do not have batteries or motors. They do not add any **energy** of their own to help people do work. So, how do simple machines work?

Simple machines work by changing the forces that are applied to them. In most cases, they do this by changing the distance or direction of a force.

## Inclined Planes

Inclined planes are sloping surfaces that connect a lower level to a higher level or the opposite.

## Lever

A lever is a moveable bar that rests on a solid point called the fulcrum.

# Pulley

A pulley is a wheel with a groove around the outside edge. In this groove, there is a rope or cable. Pulling the rope turns the wheel.

# Screw

Screws are tube-shaped tools with sharp edges spiralling around them. They are often used to fasten objects together.

# Wedge

A wedge is a triangle-shaped tool with a sharp edge. It can separate two objects, lift an object, or hold an object in place.

# Wheel and Axle

Wheels are circle-shaped objects that rotate around their center. They often have an axle in the middle to hold them in place.

# Surfing Simple Machines

## How can I find more information about levers?

- Libraries have many interesting books about levers and simple machines.
- Science centers can help you learn more about levers.
- The Internet offers some great websites dedicated to science and physics.

**The Franklin Institute has a great website for kids. Check out their simple machines page.**
Franklin Institute
http://www.fi.edu/learn/index.php

**Edheads is an interactive website which gives great examples of simple machines and how they work.**
Edheads
http://www.edheads.org/activities/simple-machines/index.htm

# Science in Action

**Build a First-class Lever**

Learn more about motion and how the fulcrum affects the force needed to move a lever.

You will need:

- an eraser
- a heavy stone, not larger than 3 inches (7.6 centimeters) wide or 3 inches (7.6 cm) high
- a ruler
- tape

1. Begin by taping the rock to the top of one end of the ruler. The rock is the load that will be moved.
2. Next, put the eraser on the table. This will be the fulcrum.
3. Place the ruler on top of the eraser. The eraser should be under the center of the ruler.
4. Push down on the end of the ruler opposite the rock. Notice how much you had to push to raise the rock off the table.
5. Now, move the fulcrum closer to end of the ruler that has the rock, and push down again. Notice how much force is needed and how far the rock moves.
6. Finally, put the fulcrum closer to the end of the ruler that does not have the rock. Push down, and notice how much force is needed to push the ruler.

# What Have You Learned?

**1** What does a lever do?

**2** Where is the fulcrum placed in a first-class lever?

**3** Where is the load placed in a second-class lever?

**4** Where is the effort placed in a third class lever?

**5** What part of a bicycle is a lever?

**6** When was Stonehenge built?

**7** How many simple machines are there?

**8** Name one example of a third-class lever.

**9** What modern building machines use levers?

**10** Who was Archimedes?

**Answers:**
**1.** A lever helps move an object. **2.** In a first-class lever, the fulcrum is placed in the middle of the bar. **3.** The load is placed between the fulcrum and the effort. **4.** The effort is placed between the fulcrum and the load. **5.** The brakes on the handlebars are levers. **6.** Stonehenge was built more than 5,000 years ago. **7.** There are six simple machines. **8.** A fishing rod is an example of a third-class lever. **9.** Cranes and power shovels use levers. **10.** Archimedes was an ancient Greek scientist.

# Words to Know

**effort:** the amount of work it takes to move an object

**energy:** power needed to do work

**equilibrium:** a state when all the forces acting on an object are balanced

**forces:** movements of pushing or pulling an object

**fulcrum:** the point where a lever turns

**hydraulics:** the movement of liquid through pipes to create force

**inclined planes:** triangle-shaped objects that connect a lower level to a higher level and vice versa; ramps

**load:** the object or substance being worked on by a simple machine

**mathematics:** the science of numbers

**mechanical advantage:** the amount of force produced by an object compared to how much is applied to the object

**motion:** movement of an object

**power:** the energy used when pushing or pulling

**pulleys:** wheels with a groove around the outside edge where a rope or cable sits inside

**rigid:** stiff and cannot be bent

# Index